Chapter 22

History Of Physiotherapy

Introduction

Overall, the physiotherapy local area is separated by name, with three distinct essential titles utilized: kinesiotherapy, physiotherapy, and physical therapy in any case, that inside the term physiotherapist, there are likewise language determinations, for example, fisio, fisicos, fysio and fiso. It will always be difficult to define the community using just one word.

According to World Physiotherapy, physiotherapy is a health care profession that focuses on maximizing physical potential and human function and movement. Within the contexts of promotion, prevention, treatment/intervention, habilitation, and rehabilitation, it aims to identify and maximize movement potential. It utilizes actual ways to deal with advance, keep up with and reestablish physical, mental and social prosperity, considering varieties in wellbeing status. It is based on science and is committed to expanding, putting into practice, evaluating, and looking over the evidence that supports and guides its practice and delivery. The activity of clinical judgment and informed understanding is at its center.

Instances of meanings of physiotherapy from around the world show that there is an agreement that 'development' is the center skill/business of physiotherapy.

CHAPTER 1

What Is Physiotherapy

In the event that you have a musculo-skeletal issue or injury, you may be given a reference to a physiotherapy facility. You know what to expect if you have been to one before. Assuming you are new to this assistance, you could ask, what is physiotherapy?

Physiotherapy is otherwise called non-intrusive treatment. That responds to the subject of what is physiotherapy for some individuals. Be that as it may, in the event that you have not had any dealings with this type of treatment, you want to know more.

A sort of medical services, physiotherapy frets about giving actual recuperating strategies to a wide range of sorts of wounds and sicknesses. A portion of these strategies are finished in an active way, by utilizing back rub or control of the musculo-skeletal framework. To receive this kind of assistance, it is essential to understand physiotherapy.

Training is a piece of what is physiotherapy. A patient will learn how to take care of their injuries from a physiotherapist. He will train activities to do at home with the goal that treatment can go on past the walls of the center or medical clinic. He will train ways of defeating troubles that can't be restored.

One more piece of what is physiotherapy is restoration. Patients have wounds from sports, fender benders, or attack. These wounds can be treated through physiotherapy. Given the right medicines and a physical issue that will answer treatment, much headway can be made. Full working might be recaptured. It might try and be feasible for them to return to work instead of being rested up at home.

A response to what is physiotherapy is what sorts of medicines physiotherapists use. Intensity, ice, and ultrasound are utilized to assuage agony and firmness. Important treatments include massage, chiropractic, and other hands-on ones. This large number of techniques will generally advance better wellbeing, both physical and mental.

Hardware for assisting patients with recovering their solidarity and versatility are a piece of what is physiotherapy. This hardware might permit an individual who is somewhat incapacitated to get the most potential activity. This is critical in keeping up with the trustworthiness of their spines and muscles.

What is physiotherapy? It is a painstakingly arranged and executed treatment system. It depends on evaluations of the circumstances that patients endure. In the event that all works out in a good way, the patient will get back to their unique condition. On the off chance that this is unimaginable, the objective is for the patient to arrive at an objective that is the best development and absence of torment that is conceivable.

Those who are referred to a clinic might be curious about what physiotherapy is. Notwithstanding, they will be offered fast responses to this inquiry. After an underlying assessment, they will be planned for medicines like ultrasound or needle therapy. They will be given home exercises to complete. A skilled physiotherapist will immediately begin treatment.

Individuals, who ask what is physiotherapy, frequently don't think about the protection side of the field. Physiotherapists encourage patients to do exercises and postures that will help them avoid physical injuries and conditions that require their services. A magnificent physiotherapist will have less return patients, however the progression of individuals requiring physiotherapy proceeds.

CHAPTER 2

What's the Connection Between Physiotherapy and Cardiac Surgery?

One might feel tired and sore after cardiac surgery; It makes perfect sense. On the other hand, the idea of starting a physiotherapy program instead of just resting seems completely out of place. However, that exactly is suggested.

Sorts of cardiovascular medical procedure incorporate detour medical procedures, angioplasty, stents, heart valve substitutions, and even heart transfers. Patients having these medical procedures can profit from physiotherapy. Patients with additional cardiac problems can also benefit from the assistance; Heart attack, heart failure, peripheral artery disease, chest pain, and cardiomyopathy victims are among them.

Physiotherapy will ordinarily start inside a long time of heart medical procedure, while possibly not sooner. The initial step is for medical caretakers or specialists to oversee a pressure test to decide how much activity one can deal with. This includes strolling on a treadmill or riding on an exercise bike while having one's important bodily functions checked.

At the point when the information is accumulated and dissected, a program of exercise-based recuperation will be instituted. For the good of security, bringing heart medical procedure patients into the emergency clinic or a short-term facility for their activity at first is in many cases the everyday practice.

During their exercise sessions, cardiac surgery patients will be cared for by nurses and physiotherapists. This way the experts will be alarmed in the event that the cardiovascular medical procedure patient is having irksome side effects. The activities done are cardiovascular activities like strolling on a treadmill or riding an exercise bike.

Patients undergoing cardiac surgery will be instructed to exercise at home following the completion of the initial phase of monitored physiotherapy. However, they will have been instructed on when to stop and how to warm up and stretch before they leave. By and large, they ought to practice three to five times each week except if they are having issues.

Swimming is one more type of activity that is particularly great for heart medical procedure patients. A cardiovascular activity isn't difficult for the joints, so it will frequently be kept up longer. The only thing to keep in mind is that every wound must first heal completely.

Physiotherapy for cardiovascular medical procedure patients is frequently not done by physiotherapy staff. Medical attendants in clinics and centers who are prepared to manage these areas of recovery for cardiovascular medical procedure will accomplish the work. Be that as it may, physiotherapists at times help, and the standards are something very similar.

The physiotherapist will train the patient about what exercises are adequate in the long stretches of time after a medical procedure. During the initial a month and a half, there might be a couple of exercises permitted, like light housekeeping or heading out to films, for instance. From that point until the third month, more exercises will be added. You might be able to drive again and return to work, even if only part-time. After this time, your physiotherapist will work effortlessly you back into all your old exercises.

A patient who undergoes cardiac surgery but does nothing to regain strength will soon become weak. A way to stay in shape or get in shape is provided by physiotherapy. By making the patient much healthier than they were before the surgery, it gives the cardiac surgery more meaning.

CHAPTER 3

What Patients with Spinal Cord Injury Can Do with Physiotherapy

Sports injuries and car accidents are two examples of injuries that can result in spinal cord injuries. Injuries to the spinal cord can occur anywhere. A portion of these wounds are genuinely minor and will mend well with a restricted measure of physiotherapy, while others need physiotherapy until the end of their lives.

As consistently with physiotherapy, the initial step is assessment. An arrangement is figured out that will incorporate treatments intended for the sort of spinal string injury the patient has. Neck wounds can cause quadriplegia, which requires exceptional medicines.

A significant issue in spinal string injury is the level of the harm. On the off chance that a physiotherapy program isn't followed reliably, the spine will start to decay underneath the level of the spinal rope injury. The spine will shrivel and the entire body underneath that point will become more fragile as time passes by.

Spinal line injury patients should get exercise of some structure. They are inclined to osteoporosis and heart issues, among different circumstances. These risk factors become even more pronounced when there is a complete lack of physical activity.

Physiotherapy for spinal string injury includes practicing and invigorating the nerves and muscles beneath the level of the harm. This will permit patients with spinal rope injury to remain in great state of being where they can. Like that, assuming that a fix opens up, they won't be too debilitated to even think about profiting from it.

Each exercise the physiotherapy staff proceed with the spinal string injury patient ought to be video-taped. This permits work to happen at home with an illustration of each activity. Scope of-movement practices are finished by a parental figure, who moves the appendages with the goal that they won't become set in one position.

For spinal line injury patients who are not quadriplegics, there is physiotherapy utilizing mats. These mats are raised off the floor, and can be worked by a hand wrench or a power framework. The physiotherapist will give practices where the patient lies as an afterthought, back, or stomach and works out or sits up and works out.

There are numerous supportive treatments in physiotherapy for spinal string injury patients. These incorporate electrical feeling, biofeedback, vibrational treatment, laser treatment and other excitement exercises. Water treatment is likewise a physiotherapy strategy that is helpful for progress in spinal line injury patients.

With this multitude of treatments, spinal rope injury patients can at times reestablish themselves to prior working. Different times, they can just hold their bodies back from decaying as they sit tight for a fix.

Spinal line injury research is being led continually. Physiotherapy is one of the fields that are being investigated. One review is placing spinal line injury patients in saddles over treadmills animating strolling. They are attempting to figure out how to assist with peopling walk again who had surrendered any expectation of doing as such.

Physiotherapy gives expect spinal rope injury patients. It permits them to have the most typical working that they are at present ready to have. Maybe when a fix comes results will be far superior. In any case, physiotherapy will likely forever be required for spinal string injury patients.

CHAPTER 4

**The Importance of Physiotherapy in Stroke Rehabilitation
Stroke rehabilitation**

can be challenging at times. After a stroke, patients can be left
with loss of motion, particularly uneven loss of motion.
Torment, as well as tactile deficiencies, must be made due.
Physiotherapy is a critical piece of the treatment plan.

Physiotherapists start stroke recovery extremely not long after
the stroke has happened, while the patient is still in intense
consideration. The physiotherapist will initially do an
assessment to figure out what incapacities should be managed
during stroke restoration.

A portion of the potential issues are: absence of solidarity and
perseverance, restricted scope of movement, issues with
sensation in the appendages, and inconveniences strolling.
Stroke recovery will zero in on the issues that the patient
showcases. An arrangement for treatment will be conceived.

Patients will figure out how to utilize appendages that the
stroke has made briefly futile. During stroke restoration, it will

be resolved whether these appendages will arrive at their past potential. On the off chance that not, the physiotherapist will train the patients ways of overseeing without their full utilization of the appendages.

One issue of stroke restoration is called educated nonuse. When this happens, people who have had a stroke try as hard as they can not to use the limbs that were affected by the stroke. In the event that left to their own gadgets, they will disable the appendage further by allowing it to decay through nonuse.

Physiotherapists use stroke restoration to ensure that patients accomplish to be sure work to utilize their debilitated appendages. They can do this in various ways. Some of the time it helps for the physiotherapist to tap or stroke the appendage they believe the patient should utilize.

Passive range of motion exercises, in which the physiotherapist moves the limb herself, can be used if the patient will not readily participate in active range of motion exercises. Different times, the patient will attempt to utilize the impacted appendage however will normally return to the appendage that is working great. For this situation, stroke recovery might include delicately controlling the sound appendages.

It very well may be a troublesome errand of stroke restoration to assist casualties with relearning changing starting with one undertaking then onto the next. This is somewhat a result of issues in the mind. The signs to move the muscles and joints to change developments are delayed in coming. Therefore, practice is so significant. The more times physiotherapists assist a patient with this, the simpler it becomes.

Late examinations have uncovered that stroke recovery can proceed with long after the clinic stay. Previously, stroke casualties were given a short round of physiotherapy during the time they were in the emergency clinic and for half a month without further ado a while later.

If physiotherapy is gradually continued at home, new research demonstrates that it can facilitate more advanced stroke rehabilitation. Patients will figure out how to walk better. They will acquire solidarity to do day to day errands. They will likewise accomplish better stance and more equilibrium, which can forestall falls.

Stroke restoration includes various treatments, all intended to reestablish capability to the patient's impacted appendages. Electrical excitement, hydrotherapy, and games have all been utilized. Physiotherapy services are essential to stroke rehabilitation.

CHAPTER 5

How Physiotherapy Can Assist with Sports Wounds

At the point when players have sports wounds, they go to physiotherapy for restoration. Physiotherapy, also known as physical therapy, helps players regardless of whether they need surgery to fix the damage.

One illustration of the many games wounds is a foremost cruciate tendon (leg tendon) injury. The knee has been hurt by this. It is one of the normal games wounds in individuals who play sports that challenge their knees, like hockey, skating, skiing, b-ball, and obviously, football. It can restrict the scope of a player's movement in that leg, and make the leg feeble.

Medical procedure is at times finished for these games' wounds, yet physiotherapy is consistently a piece of the therapy. The three significant activities done to begin the mending system of upper leg tendon are heel slides, quad sets, and straight leg raises.

Heel slides are practices for upper leg tendon games wounds that are straightforward, yet might be excruciating to do from the get go. With one foot down, one simply lies on the floor or bed. Then, at that point, one slides the foot gradually towards the bottom until it harms a bit, and slides it back. This and different activities assist with setting up the knee for medical procedure or to mend without it.

One more of the games wounds that physiotherapy is utilized for is tennis elbow. One could get tennis elbow from playing tennis, absolutely, however it can likewise happen from any action that includes turning the wrist.

Sports wounds like tennis elbow are treated with a thorough arrangement of physiotherapy. Practices are made sense of and doled out. One more typical method for sports wounds is the utilization of ultrasound. Ultrasound is an approach to applying heat profound into the muscle for relief from discomfort.

Electrical feeling can be utilized to hold torment back from being felt through the sensory system. It is utilized for tennis elbow and numerous different games wounds. Physiotherapy can also benefit from manual therapy and massage.

Rub is one of the types of delicate tissue control. Nonetheless, delicate tissue control is to muscles what chiropractic is to bones. It addresses tendons and connective tissue in addition to muscle. It is a subspecialty of physiotherapy that has frequently been utilized for sports injuries.

As many kids' games groups are turning out to be always cutthroat, sports wounds among young people is expanding. Frequently, a good-natured parent will advise the youngster to shake it off and continue to play. It is considerably more significant for kids to get satisfactory physiotherapy than it is for grown-ups. A problem in childhood can cause pain for the rest of a person's life. Children are still developing.

A few games wounds happen in light of the fact that something genuinely horrendous happens to your body. Somebody runs into you as you run with the football towards the end zone, for instance. Different times, it is just a question of the actual requests you put on your body.

Physiotherapy is instrumental in the mending of many games' wounds. Numerous elite athletics groups have physiotherapists on their staffs. Truth be told, either leg tendon or tennis elbow can become extremely durable circumstances without the utilization of physiotherapy systems.

CHAPTER 6

How Physical Therapy Helps Treat Rheumatoid Arthritis

Rheumatoid arthritis is more than just a painful and crippling condition. It is likewise a gamble factor for different infections like coronary illness and osteoporosis. Research demonstrates the way that these sicknesses can be held off by practice and other way of life changes.

For the victim of rheumatoid joint pain, life is a consistent growth opportunity. Each time another development is finished, one sees whether it exacerbates the condition or better. Rheumatoid joint inflammation patients might feel weariness. They will probably have a lot of aggravation and solidness in their joints.

Physiotherapy is one method for combatting the impacts of rheumatoid joint inflammation. Over the course of the patient's entire life, this will be an ongoing therapy that will necessitate dedication. However, it is common for the patient to be motivated to continue doing the exercises and other treatments because they have such a positive effect on the rheumatoid arthritis.

A physiotherapist comprehends how every one of the pieces of one's body cooperate to make development. Bones, muscles, joints, tendons, and ligaments: the physiotherapist knows how they generally fit to make one walk or stand. With this information, the physiotherapist can devise strategies to help one continue to move. The most crucial aspect of treating rheumatoid arthritis is this.

The strategy will take shape early on in a patient's treatment. It will include preventative measures against rheumatoid arthritis. As time passes by, the center will move to a more at this very moment kind of treatment. Activities will be equipped more towards current issues.

Water activities can be utilized for individuals with rheumatoid joint inflammation. These activities permit the individual to get genuinely necessary reinforcing and extending practices done. Simultaneously, there is next to zero tension on the joints or spine. Water exercises are an important part of the treatment plan that physiotherapists use.

People who have rheumatoid arthritis can support their joints better by strengthening their muscles through exercises. In the event that there isn't sufficient muscle tone, the patient will experience more difficulty strolling or doing other typical developments. The rheumatoid joint pain will overwhelm the developments rather than the muscles ruling them.

Heat treatment can be utilized related to ice treatment for rheumatoid joint inflammation. A physiotherapist can tell the patient when and how lengthy to leave on heat packs or ice packs. Ultrasound is used for additional heat therapy.

Individuals with rheumatoid joint inflammation can profit from manual methods, like back rub. An individual with the firmness that goes with rheumatoid joint inflammation can be extremely restricted in how far he can move his joints. Knead further develops development and builds this reach decisively.

As a motivational coach, a physiotherapist's role in the treatment of rheumatoid arthritis patients is crucial. The physiotherapist ought to be prepared in the brain science of persistent problems and agony the board. She will be there to urge you to continue on, continuing moving, and never surrendering.

Physiotherapy is just a piece of the treatment for rheumatoid joint inflammation. Diet and prescriptions are likewise utilized, for instance. However, many people with this disease would experience much worse pain without physiotherapy.

CHAPTER 7

How to Verify the Credentials of a Physiotherapist

When you receive physiotherapy, you are entrusting your body to a qualified individual. Agony and distortion could result assuming the methodology are fouled up. To that end it is smart to really take a look at a specialist's physiotherapy qualifications.

Non-intrusive treatment helpers might assume a part in physiotherapy. One isn't off the mark to get some information about what sort of physiotherapy qualifications such an individual has. The standard may basically be a two-year course of study at a Jr. School or a specialty school. However, it is critical that the center isn't simply recruiting anybody who strolls in off the road.

While physical therapy assistants can assist with some treatment tasks, the physiotherapist is the one who evaluates the patient's condition. This individual additionally designs the course of treatment and explicit medicines like extraordinary activities.

This physiotherapist is the individual to whom the patient will return for progress reports and who will supervise crafted by the active recuperation helper. It is vital to request the physiotherapy qualifications of this expert.

School coursework past the four-year college education is expected for good physiotherapy qualifications. On the off chance that a physiotherapy competitor meets every one of the necessities, a graduate degree with cutting edge preparing will set up her for work in the field.

Physiotherapy qualifications to search for are: Unfamiliar Credentialing Commission on Active recuperation (FCCPT), Worldwide Instruction Specialists (IEC), Global Advisors of Delaware, Inc. (ICD), Global Instruction Exploration Establishment (IERF), and Worldwide Credentialing Partners, Inc. (ICA). Whether or not any of these qualifications are required, the CAPTE (Commission on Certification for Non-intrusive treatment Training) is the primary accreditation required.

There are various prerequisites for physiotherapy accreditations in every one of the 50 states. Different physiotherapy credentialing offices are depended upon in various states. Some require a score of at least 600 on the permitting test. Some expect hands on preparing or proficient references from physiotherapists who notice them in preparing.

In most states, continuing education is also required to keep physiotherapy credentials current. Figure out how frequently the permit should be reestablished in your state. Then, at that point, you will know an obsolete permit when you see one. Assuming that you go into a physiotherapist's office and see an old permit, inquire as to whether that is the most current one. On the off chance that your physiotherapist can't create an ongoing permit, search somewhere else for your physiotherapy.

The state licensing board for physical therapists can be contacted to inquire about these credentials. One can find the contact data of any state's physiotherapy authorizing board on the web. In the event that nothing else works, you should inquire about the physiotherapist's certification and training. It is for her potential benefit to energize trust by being open about her physiotherapy certifications.

When it comes to requesting credentials for physiotherapy, there is no need to be suspicious or hostile. Your physiotherapist probably possesses all of the necessary skills to address all of your physical rehabilitation and problem-solving requirements. It is vital to learn about the physiotherapy qualifications, yet it is similarly as significant not to make a foe of your physiotherapist.

CHAPTER 8

Step by step instructions to Capitalize on a Physiotherapy Evaluation

The most vital phase in recuperating from a few difficult and debilitating circumstances is a physiotherapy evaluation. One can pause for a minute or two and let the physiotherapist accomplish basically everything. In any case, more exact and positive outcomes will happen to the physiotherapy appraisal assuming that the patient becomes involved.

At the point when you go in to the physiotherapy arrangement, your primary care physician ought to have provided the physiotherapist with some thought of your condition. The physiotherapy evaluation will start when the specialist takes a clinical history. For any health issue, this is the standard procedure. It is astute to be exhaustive in making sense of past issues and conditions that appear to run in the family.

This can have an orientation on your treatment. It could try and highlight some illness or confusion that nobody thought that you had. A careful physiotherapy evaluation might actually prompt treatment by a doctor for a surprising sickness. You could figure out that, while physiotherapy is awful for not many individuals, it isn't what you want the most.

Then, the specialist will pose inquiries about your current condition. She will need to know when the aggravation, solidness, or different issues began. She will ask you exactly the amount it harms, having you grade your aggravation on a size of one to ten. One method no aggravation and ten methods the most awful aggravation you can envision. Your hypotheses about what caused everything will continue the physiotherapy assessment.

The exactness of your physiotherapy appraisal lays on the accuracy with which you answer these inquiries. Let the specialist know that the aggravation is at a degree of four when you realize it is more similar to a degree of eight will lead her to treat your aggravation less forcefully. It will be as though you had no physiotherapy appraisal by any stretch of the imagination.

Notwithstanding, in the event that you can accurately quantify your level of torment, you will assist the advisor with grasping your concern. The physiotherapy assessment will reflect the therapist's knowledge of the problem's beginning date and its cause.

Then, at that point, the advisor will watch you move. For a not individual wish to be viewed as feeble, it very well might be a test to walk and do different developments as the individual does them when nobody is watching. To put it another way, someone who has a stiff neck may try to move it normally to avoid appearing weak.

You will be put through a progression of developments that might appear to be brutal to you. It is a piece of a decent physiotherapy evaluation to show every one of the developments done as best you can do them. In the event that you can scarcely do them, that tells your physiotherapist a lot of data.

The physiotherapy assessment should take into account all of these conditions and pains. The method for capitalizing on a physiotherapy evaluation is frankly and precise as could really be expected. It is really at that time that you will get the best consideration.

CHAPTER 9

Step by step instructions to Begin a Physiotherapy Profession

To help other people with actual issues, one should begin a physiotherapy profession. By doing this, you could learn how to assess physical problems, make plans for patients, and make sure those plans are carried out. A physiotherapy vocation can expertly remunerate.

The typical physiotherapist is somewhere in the range of 25 and 54, procures $50,000 to $60,000, and works in a full-time salaried position. A considerable lot of these began with a BA degree, yet the pattern is towards employing Mama certificate or doctoral certificate holders who are starting a physiotherapy profession.

If you want to work in physiotherapy, getting a degree is important. A physiotherapy helper can get a section level degree at a college, junior college, or specialized school. This is a two-year degree. After graduation, the physiotherapy assistant will perform many positions in the treatment of patients, under the heading of the physiotherapist.

To start a physiotherapy vocation as an expert, one necessity to earn either an expert's college education or a doctoral certificate. Some master's degree programs may require concurrent enrollment with college enrollment. In other places, obtaining a bachelor's degree only requires approximately three years of additional education. Doctoral certificates have comparable necessities.

Before one gets into a physiotherapy degree program, one necessity to meet explicit prerequisites. Coursework in different life sciences like science, life systems are required. Courses in areas like psychology and social science are also crucial.

To pick a school to set one up for a physiotherapy degree, it is shrewd to consider whether that school offers clinical encounters as a piece of the preparation. It is additionally vital to know about the degrees that are accessible to acquire, and the length of the course of study.

The last step prior to landing that first position to begin a physiotherapy vocation is certification. The Commission on Authorization in Non-intrusive treatment Training (CAPTE) is entrusted with guaranteeing that physiotherapists are good for the permitting test. By then, the licensure test should be taken and passed. High licensure scores impress hiring managers. When the test is finished, you are prepared to begin your physiotherapy vocation.

When the profession is begun, there will be a few interesting points. One is that many states anticipate that one should get normal updates on one's schooling. This should be possible through studios and proceeding with training courses. You cannot keep your permit without keeping up on the most recent information all through your physiotherapy vocation.

Likewise, you might need to think about a strength. There are physiotherapy vocation strengths in geriatrics, pediatrics, muscular health, neurological problems, and sports medication, to give some examples. By choosing a specialty, you increase your value, which results in a higher salary and, frequently, more respect. Other than this, you can pick a field that is the most critical to you.

You can start your physiotherapy vocation by exploring schools and finding which ones have the best projects for you. In the event that you truly do turn into a physiotherapy proficient, you will find both monetary and individual prizes look for you.

CHAPTER 10

Paediatric Problems and Physiotherapy to Help Them

It is a miserable day when one needs to manage paediatric problems in the family. The vast majority accept that kids ought to never experience the ill effects of actual issues. However, it must be acknowledged that paediatric disorders can occur. Fortunately, physiotherapy offers some assistance for them.

Sadly, there are various paediatric problems. To give some examples, there are: scoliosis, torticollis, Osgood-Schlatter, sports and horrible wounds, hesitant walkers, formative issues, cerebral paralysis, and hereditary problems.

Physiotherapy for scoliosis - a shape of the spine - comprises of activities to reinforce the back. Electrical excitement is utilized for this kind of paediatric problems. The excitement goes straightforwardly to the skeletal muscles. Chiropractic is additionally utilized with an end goal to fix the spine.

Torticollis is a type of neck disorder that affects children. There is an issue with one of the muscles of the neck so the kid can't hold his head upright. The head will be shifted aside. This jawline will extend out on the contrary side of the neck. Physiotherapy can extend this muscle so the kid can hold his head all the more regularly.

Spinal line wounds as paediatric issues are challenging to treat. Youngsters frequently don't have any desire to accomplish the work that is expected to remain in front of the weakening that can be brought about by this condition. Physiotherapy work force are tested to keep the youngster's spirits up as they show them how to practice with and without extraordinary gear.

Mind wounds, including cerebral paralysis and strokes are paediatric problems that should be overseen carefully. The neurological system is frequently weaker than the muscular or skeletal systems. Nonetheless, cerebrum wounds include these different frameworks too.

Another treatment for these paediatric problems like mind wounds is utilizing hyperbaric oxygen treatment. This kind of physiotherapy depends on the possibility that, in these circumstances, there are many times portions of the mind that are not working yet can be resuscitated. They can sometimes be revived by the HBOT.

Paediatric issues, for example, sports wounds and awful wounds require various sorts of physiotherapy in view of the area and seriousness of the injury. On the off chance that a kid has over and over hyper-extended a similar lower leg, treatment will essentially zero in on that lower leg, as well as any body part that backings or offsets lower leg. Generally speaking, strength is significant.

Horrible wounds require a specific measure of mental preparation, as the subject of the mishap or other experience might welcome on such trouble that the youngster would rather not work. A decent physiotherapist will actually want to work with such a kid. The physiotherapist may also plan a lengthy course of therapy to treat traumatized injuries if they are severe enough. Paediatric issues like this require persistence from all interested parties.

The rundown of paediatric problems is long and changed. Not every one of them might benefit from outside input by physiotherapy as of now. This moment, physiotherapy can be utilized as a rule to ease side effects or even to invert harm. Physiotherapy carries out an important role in assisting youngsters with carrying on with additional ordinary lives.

CHAPTER 11

Physiotherapy Helps Postural Issues

Postural issues have forever been an issue; In today's workplace, they are even worse. Too often individuals need to go after their PC mouse, setting them in unnatural positions. There is help for the two sorts of postural issues in physiotherapy.

Act is the way one stands, sits, or strolls. It can allude to any typical place that the body generally holds. At the point when the shoulders are slouched forward or the arm is reached out in an off-kilter position, these are postural issues. They can prompt muscle and joint torment, migraines, and other unsavoury side effects.

A few postural issues are caused in light of the fact that an individual has torment in one piece of her body. She could depend on different muscles to accomplish crafted by the ones that hurt. An unbalanced or awkward posture may result from this. In the long run, it may cause more pain.

Postural issues can be treated with physiotherapy like intensity, back rub, activities, and chiropractic control. The first step is to ease the discomfort. Patients with postural issues typically go in to the specialist with difficult side effects. Intensity can be utilized to ease sore muscles that have been holding the body in new stances.

Then, postural issues can be treated by an endeavour to switch the influence the abnormal positions have had on the muscles. Massage can accomplish this. The muscles that are fixed in view of unfortunate carriage of the body can be worked until they are less delicate.

A few muscles might have contracted, or abbreviated, because of postural issues. Different muscles which go against them could have protracted and debilitated. It is important to extend the abbreviated muscles prior to attempting to fortify, or fix, the more drawn-out muscles. Physiotherapy practices have been imagined for only this reason.

Any individual who works with a mouse that isn't sufficiently close to their console is inclined to postural issues. The initial step is to make a superior plan of the work area. Then, problems with the neck, shoulder, and wrist that come from poor posture can be fixed with exercise.

Medical procedures, similar to the Carpal passage medical procedure, are the final retreat, as physiotherapy can deal with the majority of these postural issues before such uncommon measures are required. Getting physiotherapy early on is essential if one wants to steer clear of surgery. Then, with sufficient improvement of the working environment, the medical procedure ought to never be required.

After postural issues arise, chiropractors employ physiotherapy techniques to restore the body's natural alignment. They can do controls to assist the patient with recapturing full scope of movement. They can likewise deal with the muscles to ease strain there.

Problems with posture affect people of all ages. They can all track down help for these a throbbing painfulness. Postural issues can be helped by following a strict physiotherapy schedule and changing the workplace and other settings. These patients will be able to sit and stand again comfortably with the help of the right physiotherapist. Their posture issues will not define them.

CHAPTER 12

The Alexander Strategy of Physiotherapy

The Alexander Strategy was concocted by a man named F.M. Alexander. He lived from 1869-1955. He toured Australia and Tasmania with a Shakespearean troupe as an actor. He started to generally disapprove of his voice, and the rest is history.

At the point when Alexander's throat turned out to be very dry, he got out and about of the relative multitude of specialists where he was at some random time. Not even one of them could help him. They couldn't track down any actual justification for the issue. The man refused to take no for an answer, which led to the development of the Alexander Technique.

Since there was nobody to come to his guide, Alexander started keeping a close eye on him. He invested a lot of energy investigating mirrors, attempting to figure out the thing he may foul up. He came up with a solution over the course of nine years: the Alexander Procedure.

The framework Alexander planned got the job done of reestablishing his voice. For him, this was nothing short of a miracle. As an actor, he placed the utmost importance on his voice. However, he didn't name the framework the Alexander Method. He named it essential control.

The speculation of the Alexander Method is that the head, neck, and middle are the essential variables in deciding capability, development, and stance. As such, these body parts control these highlights of the human life structures.

Through his perceptions, he discovered that by packing these body parts, the body didn't work as per its plan. For his situation, this prompted unfortunate stance, which brought about the dryness of his voice. For other people, he saw that there were different issues that the Alexander Strategy, or essential control, could help.

Essential control, as Alexander utilized it was the right situating of the head, neck, and middle with the goal that the body worked typically. Presently, the Alexander Procedure is being utilized in facilities around the country. It is educated to individuals who are youthful and individuals who are old. It is instructed to anybody comes to be educated.

Alexander Procedure experts ordinarily work with individuals on a singular premise. Gatherings can once in a while be shown the Alexander Procedure, yet this isn't standard practice. The key is for the therapist to use physiotherapy methods and provide education to help the patient use their body more effectively and function better as a whole.

The Alexander Technique is designed to facilitate muscle relaxation through physiotherapy. This is said to give individuals back the stance they ought to have had from the start. The body is worked with the human structure all in all, thus doing the Alexander Strategy is said to have impacts for all pieces of the body.

The Alexander Procedure is an exceptionally specific area of physiotherapy. This procedure resolves gives that are connected with pose just, though there are numerous issues that are. It is by and large not utilized for individuals with significant incapacities or sicknesses. Different types of physiotherapy are better for those patients. In any case, for individuals with minor issues, the Alexander Method has been known to work ponders.

CHAPTER 13

The Advantages of Physiotherapy for Tragically handicapped person Restoration

Losing an appendage is an overwhelming blow for anybody. It requires a group of experts to make the acclimation to existence without the appendage. A doctor, a prosthetist, medical caretakers, and a therapist are completely required. Add to that rundown a physiotherapy administration, which will assist with handicapped person recovery.

The advantages of physiotherapy for handicapped person recovery are various. For one's purposes, tragically handicapped people will require help in conquering apparition torments. There the appendage used to be. The sensation truly is in the nerve that would prompt that appendage assuming it were still there. This pain can be treated with the methods of physiotherapy.

Most tragically handicapped people will get a prosthetic appendage. Learning how to put it on, according to some, should be sufficient. It's anything but a programmed thing to become acclimated to a prosthetic appendage. Numerous patients have them for quite a long time while never having ordinary working with them. Amputee rehabilitation is critical because of this.

Physiotherapy can help tragically handicapped person restoration by bit by bit getting the patient familiar with utilizing a prosthetic appendage. The physiotherapy plan for this will be founded on the necessities and capacities of the patient.

The patient will likely need assistance during tragically handicapped person recovery to learn balance once more. If the affected limb is a leg or foot, this is especially true. However, having one arm that is heavier than the other may also make it difficult to balance. Physiotherapy can assist with these issues as well.

One thing individuals going through tragically handicapped person recovery really should understand is that stride is a fair plan of the fight. Even with a prosthetic leg, people won't be able to tell you have a limp if you walk correctly. Physiotherapists can teach you how to use this skill.

On the off chance that a patient has held up a drawn-out period of time prior to looking for physiotherapy after medical procedure, an issue might emerge. Certain muscles might become overdeveloped and others debilitated. This happens on the grounds that, without legitimate tragically handicapped person restoration, the patient depends on one bunch of muscles to the rejection of others. A legitimate arrangement of physiotherapy can resolve this issue.

Individuals who have lost an appendage will require an individualized activity program. Physiotherapy can give such a program during tragically handicapped person recovery. This will consider the various developments required by handicapped people to perform typical activities.

Manual treatments, like back rub, are a piece of tragically handicapped person restoration with physiotherapy. This can alleviate a lot of aggravation and strain in the muscles that are exhausted in becoming accustomed to their new circumstance. There are other options available. Heat, acupuncture, ultrasound, and electrical stimulation are a few examples.

There is a requirement for physiotherapy in tragically handicapped person restoration that no other discipline can fill. It is an essential sort of help that any individual who has lost an appendage can utilize. Because they do not believe that treatment is required, some amputees refuse it. Others feel overpowered by their misfortune. In the event that there is a method for persuading handicapped people to get physiotherapy to assist them with their restoration, they will track down recuperation a much smoother way.

CHAPTER 14

Geriatric physiotherapy is a busy field

Clinics that focus on geriatric physiotherapy never run out of work. The older have illnesses and issues in more noteworthy numbers than some other age bunch. Their consideration is troublesome, however fulfilling.

Geriatric physiotherapy turned into a specialty of non-intrusive treatment concentrate in 1989. From that point forward, physiotherapists have attempted to grasp the issues of the maturing. There is an extensive rundown of issues managed in geriatric physiotherapy.

Alzheimer's, joint inflammation, balance issues, malignant growth, cardiovascular sickness, incontinence, joint substitution, pneumonic infection, stroke, and osteoporosis are a couple of the issues covered by geriatric physiotherapy. Physiotherapists have an entire scope of treatments for these infirmities.

The kinds of issues looked in geriatric physiotherapy are assembled into three unique classifications. One class is the issues that happen on the grounds that the patient essentially doesn't utilize their appendages or doesn't work out. These issues can be tended to by reconditioning through scope of-movement practices and different activities.

Cardiovascular disease, such as heart attack and stroke, is another topic that geriatric physiotherapy addresses. The physiotherapy proficient has a variety of devices available to her to work with these circumstances. Work out, water treatment, electrical excitement, and more can be utilized.

The third class is skeletal issues. People who suffer from these conditions, such as osteoporosis and osteoarthritis, benefit from geriatric physiotherapy. These issues require unique consideration as osteoporosis makes patients frailer, and osteoarthritis is extremely excruciating.

Since falls are such an issue, the osteoporosis treatment is vital. In addition, due to its work with balance and gait, geriatric physiotherapy is responsible for preventing numerous falls. A few centers center completely around balance issues for the old.

A significant part of crafted by geriatric physiotherapy isn't pointed toward returning patients to their previous conditions of wellbeing. The main objectives are to have the option to work at their best capacities. Being able to perform routine tasks and lead an unrestricted life are valuable assets.

Likewise, geriatric physiotherapy can have a significant impact on an individual's capacity to enjoy physical activity. Golf is a movement that numerous seniors appreciate. If an elderly person is not physically able to participate, it can be a very dangerous sport. It has numerous medical advantages, as well.

Geriatric physiotherapy can zero in on actual preparation to get a more seasoned grown-up in shape to play sports like golf. This fortifies them in numerous ways. The way that it permits them to play golf will make them considerably better, both genuinely and mentally. Since discouragement is a developing issue among the old, any assist they with canning get in this space is required.

One more job of geriatric physiotherapy is to assist with recovery after knee or hip substitution medical procedures. Individuals who have these tasks are probably going to walk in an unexpected way. Their capacity to complete daily tasks and quality of life are impacted. Physiotherapists can help.

Certain individuals go to physiotherapy for the purpose of better working. Others are alluded to physiotherapy facilities by their primary care physicians for explicit issues. Still others end up in geriatric physiotherapy care in clinics or nursing homes after mishaps or diseases. These individuals might benefit from some intervention.

CHAPTER 15

The Kinds of Neurological Circumstances and Physiotherapy Utilized

Neurological circumstances might be extremely serious. They can be dangerous on occasion, and they can unquestionably influence the nature of the patient's life. There are numerous neurological circumstances and physiotherapy can help a considerable lot of them.

Alzheimer's illness removes the declining long periods of numerous more established individuals. It's surprising to learn that it can happen to people under 40. ALS or Lou Gehrig's infection is an illness that denies the cerebrum and spinal rope of the capacity to move. Physiotherapy can help with these two neurological conditions.

MS, one more of the neurological circumstances that influences the cerebrum and spinal line, can prompt a long, slow downfall. Parkinson's sickness is one more of the neurological states of the cerebrum. This one can cause shaking and loss of coordination, and issues moving and strolling. Physiotherapy offers a help to these patients.

Guillain Barre Disorder is one of the sorts of neurological circumstances that influence the mind and spinal line as well. It is an instance of the individual's own insusceptible framework going after external these regions. Requiring crisis hospitalization can be sufficiently serious. Physiotherapy offers assistance with recovering strength and adjusting to existence with the sickness.

Neurological circumstances that are immune system infections are challenging to treat. Myasthenia Gravis is one such ailment. It causes strong shortcoming in view of an absence of correspondence among nerves and muscles. Like other neurological circumstances, it tends to very incapacitate.

A lot of physiotherapy is expected to help Myasthenia Gravis patients to live with their neurological circumstances. This incorporates strength preparing, preparing in the utilization of steady gadgets, and help with normal undertakings. When working with MG patients, physiotherapists face the challenge of ensuring that excessive exercise will not improve their condition.

A significant number of the patients with neurological circumstances can't continue everyday capabilities like really focusing on themselves and their homes. It is entirely expected for these individuals to not be able to work. They might try and experience difficulty strolling or getting all over steps by any means.

Trouble gulping or relaxing; unsteadiness, unfortunate equilibrium and falls, and an all-out absence of perseverance plague large numbers of these patients who have neurological circumstances. Drugs or medical procedures can assist with a portion of their concerns, yet numerous issues are ones they should stand. Physiotherapy can offer arrangements that different parts of medication can't.

Works out, as in most physiotherapy, incorporate fortifying and extending works out. In the manner is potential, patients with neurological circumstances need to get vigorous activity. Physiotherapists might have the option to make an arrangement with the goal that this is conceivable.

Part of this arrangement for patients with neurological circumstances would incorporate equilibrium preparing and coordination preparing. With these two abilities set up, the patient will have a further developed capacity to do oxygen consuming and different activities. Sea-going activity is additionally utilized.

Patients with neurological circumstances should live with numerous issues of absence of development and capability. Physiotherapy can assist them with conquering a portion of these issues. It can make their lives simpler and more wonderful, other than.

CHAPTER 16

Sorts of Physiotherapy That Assist with bringing down Back Torment

Lower back torment plagues Americans to the degree that 80% will experience the ill effects of it eventually in their lives. It is perhaps of the most well-known reason individuals visit the specialist. For some, the issue is in excess of a passing occurrence; they need physiotherapy.

Lower back pain can be treated with a variety of physiotherapy methods. Acupuncture is quickly becoming a popular treatment for this kind of pain. The doctor places the acupuncture needles across the back while the patient lies face down. The specialist then, at that point, completes the system for lower back torment. Pain relief typically lasts for months after a series of treatments.

Rub is likewise utilized for lower back torment. The person performing the massage must be experienced in treating lower back pain. A back rub done by an undeveloped individual might cause more damage than great.

These strategies are called inactive treatments, or modalities. They are finished to the patient and not by the patient. There are different modalities that are ordinarily utilized. Intensity and ice packs are a notable type of latent physiotherapy. When a person is experiencing acute lower back pain, they can be used separately or in combination.

A transcutaneous electrical nerve trigger (TENS) can be utilized as one more methodology for lower back torment. The patient will feel the impression of the trigger rather than his aggravation. On the off chance that the TENS unit appears to function admirably for him, he will be sent home with one to use whenever it might suit him.

Acute lower back pain can benefit greatly from passive ultrasound therapy. It conveys heat profound into the muscles of the lower back. This not just eases torment. It can also accelerate healing.

Back activities might be doled out by a physiotherapist. These activities will assist with lower back torment in the event that one does them accurately and steadfastly. The only exception is when the back is in a critical condition that calls for immediate medical attention or surgery.

The activities that will assist with lower back torment the most will be relegated and directed by a physiotherapist. They might be finished at home, yet it will be important to regularly adhere to directions and check in.

These activities incorporate ones for lower back torment that stretch or expand the back and ones that reinforce it. One is an activity where one untruths inclined and moves as though swimming. This safeguards the back while giving the encompassing muscles an exercise.

Lower back torment practices called flexion practices reinforce the waist to offer help for the back. In the event that the lower back torment is decreased when one sits, these activities are significant. The first is a chest-to-knee exercise.

Oxygen consuming activity, for example, strolling is magnificent for lessening and forestalling lower back torment also. Back rub and needle therapy can be depended on to alleviate torment for most patients. Lower back pain can be alleviated and prevented by strengthening the back through exercise. Any physiotherapy that can assist with letting lower back agony will assist millions with liberating from individuals.

CHAPTER 17

Utilizing Physiotherapy to Manage Work related Injury

There is less work-related injury happening over the most recent couple of years than previously. This is part of the way in view of the impact of physiotherapy on the work environment. The principles of physiotherapy are being used to improve workplace habits and environments. They are likewise significant in managing the word related injury that occurs.

Word related injury issues incorporate back and neck issues, carpal passage disorder, shoulder and knee disengagements, tennis elbow, and leg and lower leg strains. Physiotherapy can be utilized to treat any of these circumstances.

Problems with the back and neck are common examples of occupational injuries. They occur as a result of improper sitting or lifting, turning while lifting, or repetitive turning. Laborer's comp will most likely deal with treatment in the event that the word related injury is in excess of a slight one.

Carpal passage condition is much of the time found in workplaces. In any case, it might likewise happen in different positions, for example, on sequential construction systems. Tennis elbow can be a word related injury also, happening any time one monotonously turns one's wrists. This development is much of the time done in pressing plants, for instance, as laborers bend items into holders.

Patients who suffer an occupational injury frequently receive light duty assignments. Some are even laid off. Physiotherapists can step in and assist the patients with recuperating their solidarity and wellbeing. Exercises, massage, and ultrasound are all examples of physiotherapy methods.

A physiotherapist will unquestionably give guidelines about how to do home treatment. At the point when the word related injury is adequately recuperated, the patient will be given the thumbs up to get back to work. Assuming the patient was on light obligation, he will be advised when to return to ordinary obligation. Assuming that he was off work, he will be told when he can go onto light obligation, and afterward the full everyday daily schedule.

Physiotherapy thoughts can likewise be utilized to develop a superior workplace. The work station in an office can be set up to oblige the legitimate situating of the body. This will avoid word related injury brought about by dreary developments, similar to carpal passage condition.

Word related injury brought about by off-kilter developments in the working environment can likewise be wiped out assuming that the workplace is set up in an ergonomic style. Physiotherapists have a wealth of knowledge regarding workplace design.

Physiotherapists understand what gear is best used to stay away from word related injury. Ergonomic consoles are suggested and right mouse arrangement is significant. If at all possible, the physiotherapist will recommend that you use a touch pad rather than a mouse.

Physiotherapists can be exceptionally useful in forestalling word related injury in some other sort of work environment. They might be brought in to talk with bosses and ergonomics experts about what changes should be made to make the workplace satisfactory for their patients.

Workplaces are more secure than they used to be. Ergonomics standards are utilized and by and large are legally necessary to be utilized whenever mentioned by laborers. Laborers who are harmed have great physiotherapy accessible to them. In any case, until there is no word related injury, physiotherapy will keep on having esteem in the work environment.

CHAPTER 18

What Are Physiotherapy Expenses and Will Protection Pay?

In the event that you are alluded to a physiotherapy facility for a physical issue or condition, you may be pondering the physiotherapy costs. In addition, it is essential to determine whether insurance will cover procedures and treatments. These are inquiries to respond to prior to going to the center for help.

The straightforward response is that nobody can pinpoint the specific measure of treatment an individual will require, so in general physiotherapy costs are only a gauge. It is feasible for an accomplished and gifted physiotherapist to make a genuinely precise guess of what amount of time treatment will require.

Usually, there will be a flat fee for going to the office or clinic. This covers just the essential administrations of the group. On the off chance that one doesn't give sufficient notification of scratch-off, an expense can be evaluated to recover the charge that would have been required some investment space. However, these are only the start of the charges. Physiotherapy costs go a long way past the fundamental expense.

Physiotherapy expenses can shift enormously for various treatment meetings. This is on the grounds that similar techniques are not performed 100% of the time. Some expense more than others. To get a bookkeeping of the costs for the various strategies utilized, contact the charging branch of the facility or emergency clinic. There ought to be a rundown of each kind of treatment.

Since numerous insurance agency provide patients with a selection of specialists and physiotherapists, it is insightful to examine expenses forthright. Physiotherapy expenses might influence you regardless of whether you have protection. This is particularly obvious in the event that your physiotherapist has an inclination for the overwhelming majority short visits rather than less longer ones. This will have a heading on your deductible.

Then, every one of the one needs to do is to continue to ask at every meeting what the following meeting's methodology will probably be. Along these lines, physiotherapy costs will come as little amazement to one. The main inquiry is what sort of installment courses of action will be made. Assuming the patient has no protection, all physiotherapy costs will be expected in full at the hour of administration.

Facilities frequently assist with orchestrating the installment of physiotherapy costs by reaching worker's comp or insurance agency for one. This makes it feasible for the facility to handily gather their expenses. It additionally takes the weight of calls and desk work off the patient.

Physiotherapy expenses might add up to the cost of a deductible and a little co-pay for each visit. There is a range in the number of visits, but there is a reasonable average. A couple of times each week will for the most part do the trick for four to about two months. In any case, an ongoing condition might require considerably more work.

Physiotherapy expenses can be monetarily devastating, or little change. It relies on the presence of protection or the capacity of the patient to pay using cash on hand. Protection takes care of most physiotherapy costs, however on the off chance that there is any uncertainty, don't hesitate for even a moment to inquire. Physiotherapy is there to cheer you up, not to make you stress over the amount it costs. Anything you can do to maintain the emphasis on recuperation will help you.

CHAPTER 19

What Occurs After Physiotherapy?

Physiotherapy can be a long, hard street. To persevere, one must have both willpower and endurance. The simple demonstration of keeping arrangements can be tiresome now and again. One might want to celebrate when it is everywhere; yet, what comes after physiotherapy?

The physiotherapist will pass on you with useful tidbits to trail not very far behind your physiology is finished. Something significant to remember is that any activities you are doing ought to be associated with backslides.

For instance, in the event that you dislike a vertebra in your neck, non-intrusive treatment can frequently help. However, the neck may regain its stiffness and pain after physiotherapy. Recollecting and doing the non-intrusive treatment activities might prevent the condition from deteriorating, and may truth be told lighten it totally.

You will likewise be told on the legitimate utilization of intensity packs and ice packs. You'll get a refresher course out of it, but you'll be on your own, so pay attention. After physiotherapy, you will be advised to see a doctor at the first sign of relapse.

After physiotherapy, prevention will be an important concern. The last thing you want is to need to go through the interaction once more. You can avoid physical injuries that would require you to return by taking certain precautions.

Vigorous activity is exceptionally valuable both during and after physiotherapy. It reinforces the muscles, builds oxygen to the muscles, and assists you with getting more fit. Walking, running, swimming, and cycling are all forms of aerobic exercise. Any exercise that raises your heart rate and deepens your breathing will do.

In wounds like low back torment, weight reduction can be a component. It can mean less weight on your bones and muscles. Subsequently, diet can assume a significant part in counteraction after physiotherapy. It doesn't need to be an intricate eating routine; a basic eating routine that limits food varieties, particularly the carbs and fats.

Other protection elements of life after physiotherapy include the working environment. In order to complete the task, one must acquire the appropriate movements. On the off chance that it appears to be that it is inconceivable, it is a lawful right to require an ergonomics study. Utilizing all of the ergonomically designed equipment in your workplace or office is another consideration. There might be ergonomic consoles in an extra space, in the event that you would just inquire.

One likewise needs to become familiar with one's limits. Not any more attempting to lift a 200-pound object without anyone else. After physiotherapy one realizes what can happen when one doesn't deal with one's body appropriately. It only makes sense to avoid anything that could harm you in the same way that it hurt you in the past.

Living day to day after physiotherapy might be a more wary undertaking than is was previously. One might need to think prior to acting. Regardless of what one does, it is conceivable that a re-visitation of physiotherapy will occur. The best thing to do is to put forth a valiant effort to take the appropriate actions after physiotherapy.

CHAPTER 20

How Does Physiotherapy Aid in the Treatment of Chronic Airways Disease?

Constant aviation routes infection is really a gathering of illnesses. These illnesses are likewise called constant obstructive aspiratory sickness (COPD). A patient's quality of life can significantly deteriorate as a result of chronic airways disease. Nevertheless, physiotherapy can be helpful.

Illnesses remembered for persistent aviation routes sickness are constant bronchitis and emphysema, for instance. Numerous different illnesses that confine or restrict breathing are incorporated. It is most frequently brought about by cigarette smoking, yet in addition can be brought about by breathing in different aggravations like those in the working environment. Persistent aviation routes illness is more normal among the old.

Alongside having windedness, the patient is probably going to wheeze and hack much of the time. He will create sputum in overflowing sums, and in some cases that will be streaked with blood. The lips and fingers can take on a somewhat blue color since he isn't getting sufficient oxygen, and heart inconvenience might understand for a similar explanation.

Physiotherapy can assist with constant aviation routes illness in numerous ways. One is retraining one's breathing. This is exactly what it appears to be. A physiotherapist works with the patient to train him ways of breathing that will draw the most air while killing the most wheezing. This can be an incredible assistance for those with persistent aviation routes illness.

Clapping and postural drainage are two additional techniques that physiotherapists use to treat patients with chronic airways disease. The postural seepage part is finished by situating the body with the goal that the impacted lung is over the windpipe.

Many individuals do this at home by lying on a bed and bowing the top portion of the body over it. The physiotherapist shows one how to do this so the lung will deplete. The chronic airway disease patient will soon be able to perform this procedure on his own.

Clapping is the other component of the support for people with chronic airways disease. This is finished by measuring the hand and applauding the back to slacken emissions in the chest. It is likewise called chest percussion. The physiotherapist will do this system, and will instruct it to a relative or parental figure.

Individuals with constant aviation routes infection frequently disapprove of debilitating legs. This is because they avoid walking or doing any kind of physical exercise because they have trouble breathing. The objective of physiotherapy for this situation is to reinforce the legs through treadmill-strolling or fixed cycling. This must be finished, notwithstanding, assuming the patient is alright to begin.

Molding the arms of ongoing aviation routes infection patients is comparably significant. Most day-to-day positions depend vigorously on the arms to accomplish the work. Practices which center around the arms not just fortify the muscles of the arms. They additionally help the patient beginning breathing better.

Constant aviation routes illness is a condition that can profit from physiotherapy. For this kind of treatment, the physiotherapist treating the patient needs to have specialized knowledge. Straightforward strategies can be ignored as present-day medicines come to the very front. However, physiotherapy work force who realize this method can have a major effect in patients' lives.

CHAPTER 21

Advantages OF PHYSIOTHERAPY

We are posting underneath certain circumstances where physiotherapy has helped in giving the most ideal outcomes.

Wiping out or diminishing agony

Patients experiencing joint pain, muscle strain/sprain or tendonitis benefit from utilizing helpful procedures and activities, for example, Delicate Tissue Activation or utilization of modalities like TENS, IFC and Ultrasound. These treatments help in reducing the aggravation consequently guaranteeing business as usual. You can check with our particular and prepared physiotherapists at Etobicoke place for more data on this.

Helps in staying away from a medical procedure

We should confront this. We are all living through difficult pandemic conditions, and no one wants to go to the hospital or have surgery. Be that as it may, there are a few undeniable circumstances where medical procedure is the final hotel. Physiotherapy can help in staying away from this by overseeing and mending in the underlying stages itself. It is additionally useful in pre and present recovery programs on moderate the difficulties that can happen in the medical procedure. Before planning a surgery, we recommend consulting our Toronto physiotherapists if you live in or near Toronto. If you are currently recovering from surgery or treatment, you can also talk about your case.

Working on generally speaking strength and coordination

While physiotherapy is profoundly helpful to diminish the aggravation during or after a medical procedure, it likewise supports working on the general strength and vigor of the body. Do you have any idea about that physiotherapy includes explicit activities and stretches that assistance in aggregate coordination of the body? Along these lines, in the event that you are confronting side effects of dizziness or wooziness, we propose you to reach out to our Physiotherapists. Our highly qualified physiotherapists in Oakville can tailor a program to meet your needs.

Decreasing the reliance on medications

Each medication that a patient consumes has a secondary effect sooner or later throughout everyday life. Certain circumstances request a patient to take prescriptions to control or treat his/her condition. Nonetheless, there are cases like a medical procedure, where a patient is subject to the medication for help with discomfort. We recommend physiotherapy as an elective decision to address this worry and lessen the reliance and aftereffects brought about by medications.

Supporting cardiovascular working and lung limit

Post-stroke a medical procedure requires intense consideration and recuperation program. Physiotherapy offers post heart stroke patients in recovering their certification and ability to know east from west, development and equilibrium. Our experience physiotherapists at Triangle Physiotherapy helps the patients in correcting to their everyday solid way of life. You can counsel our carefully prepared and best physiotherapists at Lawrence Park for unique projects on breathing activities that assists in reestablishing the ideal lung limit and blood with streaming in the body.

Overseeing and forestalling sports related wounds

We comprehend that sports is about spryness and different games can raise the gamble to explicit kinds of conditions like upper leg tendon Tear, Golf players Elbow, Hamstring strain to give some examples. Physiotherapy is critical and valuable in such circumstances as it gives unmistakable treatment to work on the perseverance and fix the suggestive issue. Other than the wounds, sportsperson and competitors are benefitted with normal physiotherapy meetings. Our group of talented physiotherapists at North York helps in working on the dissemination and reinforcing body muscles. This builds the adaptability which will further develop whichever game you play.

Remaining fit at all ages and stages

Advanced age isn't wonderful all the time. It carries with it certain confusions that hamper the day to day way of life. These incorporates Rheumatoid Joint inflammation (RA), Osteoporosis, Sciatica, Dementia, Neck torment, Back torment,

Knee substitution and so forth. This large number of infirmities can be controlled and overseen by physiotherapy. Assuming that you or any of your friends and family is confronting advanced age issues like these, we recommend you to actually take a look at our restoration facility across GTA. You can examine Triangle Physiotherapy Mississauga or some other center near your area.

Overseeing heart and diabetic circumstances

It has been many times seen that the diabetes patient experiences the ill effects of inconveniences like knee, shoulder and back torment. This is frequently come about due to the lopsided sugar levels in the body. Diabetes-related pain management can be helped by specialized physiotherapy plans. These plans likewise help in controlling the sugar levels. Our master physiotherapists at Triangle Physiotherapy help in directing the patients about Diabetic Neuropathy, Diabetic Foot and so on.

Facilitating pregnancy and post pregnancy care

Pregnancy is a wonderful excursion. Nonetheless, numerous ladies face inconvenience in this excursion as their bodies go through basic changes affecting by and large prosperity and wellbeing. Numerous ladies face issues like fluctuating chemicals, trouble in completing routine exercises because of expanded body weight, addressing propensities and so forth. We propose checking with our splendid physiotherapist in Sovereigns Quay facility to partake in this awesome experience

Improving mental health

Mental health is the most important of all the amazing benefits of physiotherapy. We are not saying this simply as far as 'feeling blissful and great'. We comprehend that psychological wellness is significantly more than that. At Triangle Physiotherapy, we recognize and advocate the way that feeling better in your body is significant to finish your day-to-day tasks, yet in addition to raise your trust in anything that do and any place you go. That is the reason we are - to assist you with understanding your valid and maximum capacity.

Chapter 22

History Of Physiotherapy

Doctors like Hippocrates, and later Galenus, are accepted to have been the main specialists of physiotherapy, pushing rub, manual treatment procedures and hydrotherapy to treat individuals in 460 B.C.After the improvement of muscular health in the eighteenth hundred years, machines like the Gymnasticon were created to treat gout and comparable illnesses by precise activity of the joints, like later advancements in physiotherapy.

Shoulder Rubs: Help at Gallery in Cyrene Libya remembered to be 2000 years of age

The earliest reported starting points of genuine physiotherapy as an expert gathering date back to Per Henrik Ling "Father of Swedish Vaulting" who established the Imperial Focal Organization of Tumbling (RCIG) in 1813 for back rub, control, and exercise. In 1887, PTs were given authority enrollment by Sweden's Public Leading body of Wellbeing and Government assistance.

Soon after, other nations followed. In 1894 four medical attendants in Extraordinary England shaped the Contracted Society of Physiotherapy. The School of Physiotherapy at the University of Otago in New Zealand in 1913, and Reed College in Portland, Oregon, in the United States in 1914, which produced "reconstruction aides" as graduates.

Research catalyzed the physiotherapy development. The main physiotherapy research was distributed in the US in Walk 1921 in The PT Audit. Mary McMillan established the Physical Therapy Association, which is now known as the American Physical Therapy Association (APTA), in the same year.

Treatment through the 1940s essentially comprised of activity, back rub, and footing. Manipulative methodology to the spine and limit joints started to be polished, particularly in the English Republic nations, in the mid-1950s. Sometime thereafter, PTs began to move past clinic-based practice, to short term muscular facilities, state funded schools, school/colleges, geriatric settings, recovery focuses, clinics, and clinical focuses.

Specialization for exercise-based recuperation in the U.S. happened in 1974, with the Muscular Segment of the APTA being framed for those actual advisors spend significant time in muscular health. Around the same time, the Global League of Muscular Manipulative Treatment was formed,which plays had a significant impact in propelling manual treatment overall since.

Physiotherapy is been around for over 2000 years and has only gotten better.

So, there is a lot more that what can be covered in one book.

This book by now would have opened doors for you that you didn't know existed. now with more understand you can make better decisions.

Thank You for Reading

Take More Than Good Care

Until Next Time

With More Than Love From (MODERN SAVIOUR)